K. Lee

THE

ECSTASY

You want Heaven...
But won't Give Up
HELL

THE ECSTASY

All rights reserved. No part of this book may be reproduced or transmitted in any form or by any means, electronic or mechanical, including photocopying, recording or any information storage and retrieval system without written permission of the publisher except for brief quotations used in reviews, written specifically for inclusion in a newspaper, blog, magazine, or academic paper.

Published by Krystal Lee Enterprises (KLE Publishing)
Copyright © 2016 by K. Lee All rights reserved.
Please send comments and questions:

Krystal Lee Enterprises
1007 Green Street Suite SE #1635
Conyers GA 30012

www.KLEPub.com   770-240-0089 Ext 1
krystalleeenterprises@gmail.com

Printed in the United States of America.

ISBN: 978-0-9971378-4-2
Library Control (PCN) #: 2016918614

CHAPTERS:

Foreword………………………………........ 5

Introduction…………………………………8

Who Gives you The Power…..……………... 12

He Wants it All ……………………………….. 23

Don't Fight, You Wont Win ………………… 33

Trust And Open Your Eyes…………………… 45

Holy Spirit Revelation: Serve ……………..... 56

Examine Yourself…………………………… 70

You're Not Hopeless …………………….... 81

About the Author……………………….….. 93

Connect With Krystal Lee. ……………….... 97

Other books by KLE Publishing . ………….... 98

FOREWORD

We live in a world where life has many believing we can have our cake and eat it too! In years previous, the statement was made that the two can't be done, but now people say it with a giggle and that's their expectation. To not be able to eat the cake that you make, may feel like you are cheating yourself. To date, many struggle with controllable weight, health, life, social, and romantic problems.

This concept does not just plague our eating habits but curb our life experiences. If you believe everything you have is yours, the concept I am my brothers keeper is foreign and many are like Cain. Am I supposed to care for my brother? Why? He/she is able to work, go to school, have parents that provide, is it my fault that they didn't make better choices?

The short answer "no" it's not, but that problem will impact your family with the longer you live. The more time spent on earth one will recognize if you keep bread from the people in the valley, sooner or later, they will visit your vineyard. These people will take what they don't have not to be cruel, but to survive. So if one can make better decisions that can impact their lives for the better, and help others in the process, do it and deny the ecstasy that only pleases oneself.

INTRODUCTION

We live in a world where our thoughts, ideas, virtues, morality is constantly being challenged. People want to know how, when, why you believe what you believe; and if possible some want to change you. Some people feel if you don't have this inclusive acceptance of all things man decided to do—except for the "generally bad things," you are an offbeat thinker and need to be awakened.

This book entitled "The Ecstasy" talks about what happens when you give your life over to the ecstasy. What you find is the ecstasy is a trap to rob you of your heavenly appointed talent, entitlement, and connection with the Creator of the Universe, aka Adonia, The Great One, YHWH (Yahweh).

I encourage you to read this book and apply the information if relevant, but mostly share this book and the contents found to help those around you. I know sometimes it is hard to be the bearer of bad news, but the truth is: "We carry the Good News!" The Good News doesn't always make people feel warm and fuzzy on the inside but it will change their life.

If you or people you know are tired of living life crazy, unfulfilled, in addiction, broken, in bondage, it is time to break the chains off your thinking, your belief, and embrace the Living

Word that has power. The world an especially the young generation has become convinced you can make it through life on sheer will power, education, and facts absent of miracles, power, and Yahweh.

I assure you that life, breath, and every good thing is in the power of Yah's hand. Don't lean on your own understanding. Read this book and discover in a simple way, what Adonia

has to say about the state of the union—the world He created.

WHO GIVES YOU THE POWER?

What a valid question. Many wonder and ask the question, regardless if they verbalize it, who or what gives you the power to say anything to me or about me? I tell you that I am not your judge but only a messenger. I am not hear to condemn you but the truth be told, you are condemned already if you don't believe. Allow me to explain.

The Mosaic Law was giving in the Old Testament. The law was written so that man would have a moral compass on what is virtuous, good, and acceptable to Yahweh the Creator. In knowing the law, we find no man created under heaven is found perfect, possible to complete the law, or escape condemnation. All men have fallen short of the glory of YHWH (Romans 3:23).

"What a cruel Creator," some would argue to give a law He knew no man could keep out of his own being. The follow up question, however, how would man know how worst off he was if there were no law? Can you imagine what life would be like with no law, in baby terms, no rules? If everything you say, you thought goes, how selfish, sad, corrupted, and heartless would the world instantly become?

Have you ever noticed a child doesn't have to be taught to be selfish? Children are born with natural desires to eat, sleep, burp, and pass waste. These functions are not taught but are innate to the child. When the child cries he/she understands that gets results. So a form of communication instantly learned, crying, screaming gets results.

A baby must then learn a language, mannerism, acceptable behaviors and unacceptable actions to function in society. Can you imagine your quality of life if you never learned these critical components? You would be crying, fussing, fighting about everything that doesn't go your way. You would believe everything you think and do is right, because a baby knows everything—according to them.

"Unless you are like children you will never enter the Kingdom!"

A willing spirit still has to be like a baby to learn or we will lean on our own understanding and never grow—never mature. Immature teenagers, some argue middle schoolers, are some of the most difficult to teach. They are not quite children neither are they adults, but are in between. Some in this growing group is convinced they know enough to function as an adult and need no more training. Or perhaps they are smart enough to pick what training they think they need.

Have you ever met someone who can tell you everything, but when you try and help them, they tell you they don't need anything from you? People are quick to tell you I know my faults but you need to learn what yours are. The repo man and the bank, are only doing their job should you encounter them, they're the messenger but are not the source.

Too many times we hate the messenger not realizing what we need to hate is the source. The source in this example is poor money management. How many of our problems are related to our poor decision-making? In other cases we hate the source that created the rules, i.e. the bank or the car lean holder. The Bible says, "It is not I who you hate but my Father who sent me (John 5:23)."

In our world, society, same as old, we have people who want to function autonomous to the natural order. The natural order to some is up for debate, but science and belief tells us otherwise. There is a natural order that when followed will create life, set positive boundaries, and all can function in harmony. When we buck at the system, reject the natural order we have chaos, death, non-uniformity and every wicked thing.

Although many may choose not to accept the Lord's authority—The Great I AM, that does not negate His Word. When the Lord founded the earth He said man and woman shall procreate. He said that women are to respect their husband and husbands are to love their wives (Ephesians 5:33). He set the foundation to what is good and acceptable. What is sin and not sin (James 4:17). He is the governing authority as long as His essence is in the earth.

There will come a day and time where the Lord will remove His essence from the earth and the hedge of protection around His children would no longer be necessary because His children aren't here (1 Thessalonians 4:13-17). The Lord said to seek me while I still may be found (Isaiah 55:6-7). Meaning, if you seek my TRUTH now, you are prepared to fight the only battle there is for us to fight, the Ecstasy.

The Ecstasy is temptation. Temptation offered by satan and his legion, are crafty offers, tricks, and lies sent to distract you about what you are called to be, do, and become. The devil is crafty and he is not capable of friendship because his only loyalty is to his revenge.

"The devil has no Friends!"

Before there was an Adam there was a satan. He had a job to watch over the earth and he loved his job, his freedom. Being entrusted with such a position he never thought that some day it would be taken from him and given to another. He thought he was a king, a god over the land the Lord only asked him to keep watch over. When the Lord decided to bring man and give him dominion over earth the devil wasn't happy.

He hated man and thought he knew enough to be the Lord's equal but he was not. He was cursed and condemned. The third of heaven that left the heavenly realm to follow satan were also judged (Revelation 12:7-12). The devil and the fallen angels never liked man because when they wanted to repent for their evil decision the Lord forgave them not. So why do they hate you?

They hate man because they are able to repent and find favor in the Lord's eyes while they cannot ever return from where they choose to leave; the presence of the Most High. They are forever separated from his Almighty Presence and this is Hell. Some may think hell is on earth, I can understand the reasoning. If you are on drugs, unloved, abused, and living day to day in what may appear to be hell, but this, however, is not hell.

Hell is the permanent separation from the Most High. If you are on earth you can choose to seek His face. You can choose to hear the preacher. You can choose to repent, stop doing that sin, and take on YHWH's thoughts and then you will receive the healing you need (1 John 1:9, 1 Chronicles 7:14). The healing can be for your body, mind, spirit, and your soul.

The Lord is able to handle any problem because no problem is too big. But the devil tries to get all humanity to believe that the Lord doesn't care for them. He is not all-powerful and could care less if you live or died. Believers know and understand that it is not the Lord's will that any man shall perish and go to hell (2 Peter 3:9). Hell, eternal fire, death, hurt, pain, and separation from the Great I Am was never in the plan for us.

The devil tempted Adam and Eve to chase the ecstasy, the desire, craving to be like the Creator. He told them they would be knowledgeable

able to make their own path, choose their own way, design their own destiny. Adam and Eve tried to outwit the Lord and ended up playing out the plan of the devil because they gave into the ecstasy, a fleeting moment that appeared to be good, but lead to death.

All sin in its time gives you a high, ecstasy, but what happens when sin grows? What happens when you wake up the next day and realize—if you are in tune to hearing the Holy Spirit? You feel convicted; you know you erred, but what then? Do you embrace your high? Allow the devil to guilt trip you into continuing in your path of destruction? Or follow the Lord's advice and confess your sin, repent, and not return?

The Lord says my ways are not yours, my thoughts are not yours—they're higher. The Lord expects man to come up to His way of thinking, to exchange our thoughts, will, for His. One thing we are all going to realize in life the battle is not in flesh and blood but against powers of darkness and demons in high places (Ephesians 6:12). There are only two kingdoms, the Lord's and not the Lord's. If you don't choose His kingdom, you have chosen not to be in His kingdom.

People don't have a kingdom outside of what the Lord provides. For His children He provides heaven and a new earth; and for those not His, He pro-

"There are no kingdoms except the ones the Lord creates!"

vided hell. The devil is not the god over hell, he is simple a permanent resident like he tries to get every man to be also.   The Lord controls all kingdoms, but resides in heaven and in His children.

The Bible says believers are the temple of YHWH (1 Corinthians 3:19, 6:19). If we are the temple of the Most High, then we must present our bodies as a living sacrifice, holy and acceptable unto our Father (Romans 12:1). If we are not willing to present our bodies for honoring the Lord, then we provide our bodies for dishonor.

Providing your bodies for dishonor means you don't allow the Father of Life to take residence in your life, but the father of death, destruction, wickedness, and every lewd thing. There are only two fathers, the Father of Life and the father of lawlessness (John 5:26). One brings life and every good thing and the other brings death and destruction.

Fresh and salt water cannot flow out of the same vessel and neither can man expect to be a beacon of light and choose to live in open opposition to the Lord. If He dwells within your temple, then you must know, practice, and live out His ways in your lifestyle. In Him are we to live, breath, and maintain our being and if we don't, do we really believe—are we truly converted (Acts 17:28)?

An empty prayer does not move the Lord. Words spoken out of obligation, not in spirit and in truth, do not resonate with the Father of heaven. What He wants is for us to repent, turn away from sin, seek His face through prayer, studying, and renewing our minds; He says then He will hear us, forgive us, and heal our land (1 Chronicles 7:14).

If we are not willing to do as the Lord commands we cannot expect Him to move on our behalf. Emotions don't rule over Him neither is He fooled by our lies. He sees and knows who our father is because He knows our hearts (Jeremiah 17:10). So who gives anyone the power to correct wrong doing in your life? What entitles people to say there is a standard and that your standard is wrong—or right?

The Lord who has created everything under the sun is that divine and powerful authority. No one can make Him change His mind or be His council (Job 15:8). If you were born a male or female, you cannot say the Lord made a mistake and you were supposed to be this or that because the Lord does not lie (Numbers 23:19).

You cannot say that the Lord wanted me sick, broken hearted, suffering, when the Lord tells us that sin brings death, pain, and torment.

> *"The Lord is not a man, so He does not Lie!"*

These conditions are not from the Lord but are from the father of lies, the kingdom of darkness, and the Lord opens his arms and hands to defend us.

He gave the life of Yeshua, a perfect sacrifice, so that we will have communion with Him. We don't have to pray through a saint, but come boldly to the thrown of grace and make our petitions known to the Almighty Creator of Heaven and Earth! For those that believe the Lord is capable of error, makes mistaking, telling lies, I ask, "Who has bewitched you (Galatians 3:1)?"

For those believing there are multiple ways to heaven and no matter how you live your life you can make it into heaven, you are wrong. Again I ask, "Who has bewitched you?" The Lord is holy, awesome, and fearless and He said beside Him there is none

"I am the Way the Truth and the Life!"

(Isaiah 44:6). He searched to and fro and found none greater nor equal to Him (1 Samuel 2:2). The Lord can defy time, energy, matter, space, and everything known to man and what is not known to us, is known by Him.

The Bible says in Joshua 24:14, "Choose this day who you will serve?" There is a choice all man have to make, to serve the Lord or to serve the darkness. Both are looking for a temple.

Both desire a vessel here on earth to work out their plans. A vessel for honor or dishonor you will become and the choice is yours. As long as your body has breath you can choose to be a beacon of light or darkness. What you can't be is a beacon of both!

HE WANTS IT ALL

It is often quoted we serve a jealous God but what triggered the trend? The Great I Am in Exodus 34:14 says in the NKJV "For you shall worship no other god, for the LORD, whose name is Jealous, is a jealous God." In the KJV version it says, "For thou shalt worship no other god: for the LORD, whose name is Jealous, is a jealous God." In both versions and in all translations we can understand that the Lord of heaven is "jealous."

He is jealous over His people and consistently in the Old and New Testament He instructed them to listen and obey Him. Like a mother and child, a mother knows her child loves her not by what he/she says, but by what is done. When parents find out their children are acting up in school, disobeying authority, and etc. her biggest pain is not in the mistake, but that the child didn't listen or value their advice.

It pains the Lord when we deny Him His power and glory. He says His love is inseparable from us and He will never leave nor forsake us (Hebrews 13:5). The question then becomes, do we as believers believe Him and trust His promises? Or do we doubt His power, mercy, and Word? If you are not fully convinced that the Lord is your source, you will attempt to half step and live in this gray space; which doesn't exist.

For example, there is a woman with a child in a relationship that is breaking down, abusive, and far less acceptable than the Lord designed. Nowhere in the Bible does the Lord support beating your wife, girlfriend to keep her in line; that is man made.

If this woman stays with this person, knowing she is a child of the Most High, she doubts the Lord's Word about her. She questions, or second-guesses if He may have been applying His truths to her or to people in general. She cannot believe He is sincere about her, because if she did she would have no fear, and would leave a damaging situation because it displeases her Lord.

If being with someone causes you to sin or live in sin, it is not pleasing to the Lord. We must not be confused that the ecstasy is what we are chasing. The ecstasy is not always a loving high; sometimes it is a devastating one.

When we know going down a path is imminent death, we are either choosing to commit suicide or we doubt our path leads to death. If we are told that sin leads to death, we either commit spiritual suicide, or we don't believe (James 1:15).

Many believers struggle with their prayer life, seeing positive change, or the Hand of Adonia in their lives because they doubt His hand exist or will work for them. The Bible says a double-minded man can expect nothing from Him (James: 1:7). He further says, "A double-minded man is unstable in all his ways (James 1:8)." If you doubt the power of the Truth in the Bible it will not work for you.

People can believe in principles, Bible truths, and choose not to believe in the Lord. Thinking, one may say how can that be possible seems like a contradiction. But reaping and sowing is a lasting principle (Galatians 6:7). A clear way of understanding this principle in the world is tax season. All year long faithful believers give and so does the world.

At the beginning of the year these people are issued tax breaks, finances, and gifts for the money they offered to help the Lord's Kingdom or bless others. The Bible says the wheat and the tares will grow together (Matthew 13:30). What that means is believers and unbelievers can enact principles but only those that trust in the promises of the Most High can receive the promise and the gifts from the Almighty. Faith is the currency of heaven.

Without faith it is impossible to please the Creator of Heaven and Earth (Hebrews 11:6). The Lord is not interested in your words, your emotions, your ideas, but interested in the very core of your being. He wants it all from us. Why? Why does the Lord demand that we give Him our life (Romans 12:1)? The Lord demands our life because He first gave His Word, His Son for us (1 John 4:10).

"Faith is the currency of Heaven!"

The Lord became the sacrifice we all needed

and lived a life none of us could live. Our Heavenly Father gave His Son as a holy, perfect, and honorable sacrifice to redeem all men (Hebrews 10:14). He was the Second Adam that redeemed all men from how the First Adam caused all men to fall victim to the curse and the Law. Yeshua fulfilled the Law so that we all can break free and get beyond the veil.

We think it is cruel of Him to demand our lives, but miss how our selfish way could choose not to follow Him. If you were dying on the side of the road, you had a bad crash and the people that hit you drove off and left you for dead. You know satan and the angels of darkness have no friends, so after they use you up they release you hoping you die in your sins.

Believing that the precious gift of mercy, forgiveness, and salvation you wont realize or accept. But you hear the Word of the Lord whispering, shouting, and speaking lovingly in your ear. At this time, you are uncertain of what voice it is, where it's coming from, but you trust that it is here to help you. You say yes to the voice, I want help, and you follow it.

Minute by minute, hour by hour, day by day, month by month, you get better—stronger. Then you are healed; regardless of if it is internal, mental, social, physical, or financial. You are freed and set on a new ground but what you do next demonstrates your true allegiance. It is not when we are in our weakest moments we find out who we are, but when we think we are strong.

You see the whole world believed in YHWH after 9/11. The whole world asked for His healing hand when earthquakes, hurricanes, typhoons, and other natural disasters ravish lands. But do we call on Him when the weather is fine?

How about when our bodies appear healthy, finances are good, and life is well? We host carnival, we celebrate the day of the dead, we drink beyond our limits; we are promiscuous, lusting after the flesh and a gambit of things. We disregard our elders, authority, and abuse our power.

We are selfish in our actions and selfish in our thoughts. We are being lead astray because we chase the ecstasy in life. We want the high and don't think about the low. The low is sin brings death. The Bible says "No good thing would the Lord keep from you (Psalm 84:11);" but the opposite is true about the devil. Every good thing will he try to keep from you and your family.

Yes, our choices not only affect us but also affect others around us. As believers we don't make up a unit, we make up a body—a kingdom. If we are not willing to fulfill our function the entire body suffers, is sick, and does not perform to its optimum ability. The Lord's will is not that we don't fulfill our purpose, but that we allow Him to finish the work He started in us (Philippians 1:6).

If we don't yield our entire being to the Lord, we are choosing to operate out of flesh and not Spirit. Operating out of flesh is being a puppet in the devil's territory. Humans, women or men, is no match for sin. If we were, Yeshua did not need to die for us because we could have saved ourselves. The very fact that we needed a savior and that He was provided proves how the Lord loves us. What does our life choices prove about us?

Do we love the Lord or do we love the high of sinning more? It is a choice we must make and to make no choice, or to not choose the Lord's way, is to choose the flesh. Some call the flesh choosing themselves—their way; others call it humanism or Satanism. The first law of Satanism is to do what you want to do. If you are hell bent on doing what you want to do, you are fulfilling the first law of worshipping the devil.

Don't allow the devil to deceive you that choosing to do what you want to do is not demonic. It is; and what makes it so is because you have removed the Almighty from being your god and placed yourself there. You have made your own idol, and the idol is you!

You worship, bow down to yourself, and put your thoughts above *"Put no other gods before Me!"* His thoughts. Man's thoughts are inferior to the all powerful YHWH. When you choose to worship yourself and be like the Most High, you are acting like your father, who wanted to be like the Most High and also failed (Isaiah 14:14). The devil can't teach you how to win only how to loose—and big, because that is what he has done. He lost it all and his number one goal is to insure you loose it too!

The Lord is the Creator and He brings life!

When you allow your flesh to be weak, it is then the Lord is made strong (2 Corinthians 12:9). Your spirit man should guide, rule, and keep your flesh. The two are not friends and will always challenge each other because they serve two different kingdoms. The flesh will look for the high, the ecstasy, and the spirit of a believer will long to please the Lord (Galatians 5:17).

To please the Lord we must empty ourselves. We must let go of our ideas, plans, desires, thoughts, and take on those of Christ! If we are not willing to give up everything to serve the Lord, the Bible tells us we are not worthy of the promise (Luke 14:26-33). If we don't see the value, appreciate the gift of Christ, we cast priceless pearls before swine; the Bible tells us not to cast our pearls before swine (Matthew 7:6)!

We are the temples of the Most High and yes that is a gift to be in the presence of Him (Acts 7:48). How many of us have given our gifts to swine? Have trusted a man or a woman with our heart, being, money, time, only to end up with nothing? We are all guilty of given our selves to swine. If we have given our lives to the ecstasy whatever that maybe for you, sex, corruption, money, adultery, fornication, lust, drugs, gluttony, homosexuality, transgender, and the many more examples, we have all given our pearl to swine at one point and time.

But if the Lord had no plan then we would all be doomed because all men, women have sinned and fallen short of the glory of YHWH

(Romans 3:23)! The Good News, we all can be saved if we choose to accept the gift of salvation. If we accept the gift of salvation we too can be redeemed. The Lord said He is a redeemer of time (Ephesians 5:16). Not only will He redeem the time we lost but also make us whole!

The Bible says, those who He has made clean are clean indeed and no man, devil, or angel of darkness can tell us otherwise (Acts 10:15). Don't let people pull you back into sin. Don't allow the devil to convince you that once you have been born again, made clean, made whole, that you are not worthy or capable of living a righteous and holy life. We are more than conquerors because of Christ (Romans 8:31-39)!

We must believe that we are the vessels of the Lord and live accordingly because if not we loose! If we doubt the Word we cannot be angry, shocked, disappointed when it doesn't work for us. Yeshua said because of your faith, you are made whole (Mark 5:34). If you have no faith, you have no heavenly currency. If you have no currency how can you obtain anything in this world or the next?

ATMs don't kick out money if you have no currency and neither can you make a withdrawal from our Heavenly Father without currency. Faith is the currency of heaven and unless you use your faith to yield your sword, raise your shield, put on your helmet, and place your breastplate, you are not fit to serve or receive. No soldier in this day or times past will enter a war without a weapon or a shield. You must be able to activate the Word!

The Lord wants it all because fresh and salt water cannot flow out of the same vessel (James 3:11). If you are neither hot nor cold, you are good for nothing because you are lukewarm and the Lord will spit you out (Revelation 3:16). Choose whom you will serve and don't try and have religion, a form of godliness and no power; it yields you nothing but vain glory (2 Timothy 3:5).

"Be Hot or Cold but Never Lukewarm!"

The Lord is great and jealous; He will share His glory with no one. So the moment we step out from the Lord's protection don't be surprised if we are quickly wounded, fall, or die because we lost our protection. The Lord is our protector, our provider, friend, and the Creator of the Universe. I can think of no other more worthy of my all and yours.

DON'T FIGHT, YOU WONT WIN

It is never easy fighting the Most High, boxing with the Lord, or even trying to out wit Him. Rest, it's impossible. Many that are mistaken to believe they can take out the Lord don't know some critical elements to His character. The Lord is complete in Himself!

Unlike the Lord, man seeks a source, a power that keeps feeding constant power. We are like various lamps, TVs, radios, washers, dryers, and microwaves but without the power, these gadgets have no power—no life. They simple exist and take up space.

Although man would like to believe we have an autonomous power, we must first understand matter is not neither created nor destroyed. If matter cannot be created nor destroyed, how did it come into being? Something started the solar system, set up the stars, created the first animal to initiate a reproduction system. Nothing just came into being out of thin air! It came into being because the Great I Am Spoke life and nothing in this realm or beyond can deny Him.

The Bible teaches us a rock, a tree, the earth obeys and worships the Lord. If we wont celebrate

Him a rock will worship the Lord in our stead (Luke 19:40, Romans 8:22)! The Lord should not and does not have to beg us to respect, love, nor worship Him. The galaxies are indebted to His Word. The Word we know by Yeshua, some reference Him as Jesus, but His divine name is Yeshua!

Yeshua is the Word born in flesh (John 1:14). He is the embodiment of every Word that the Lord speaks, the living Word (James 1:22). The listeners of a young Christ, age of 13, were perplexed at His knowledge and understanding of the Word (Luke 2:39-52). They contemplated how He was so advanced and who trained Him? He did not need to be trained on the Word because He is the Word!

Why do you have to be trained on the essence of your being? Everything that is, is, because of the Word. The Word was here before time, before man, before satan, demons, and anything beneath the Lord Almighty. Everything is subject to the Son because everything is because the Lord ushered their existence through Him (1 Corinthians 15:27).

The Word is more than a man, He is the Mouth Piece, the Power, and He abides in the Most High! The Bible says in John 14:20 that Yeshua abides in the Lord Almighty and He abides in Him (John 15:4). With us, the Lord dwells in our being occupying our vessel, we do not occupy His vessel. Man is beneath the Creator.

"The Student will never surpass the Master!"

The Bible said the student is never above their teacher (Luke 6:40). Although people can be little "gods," we can never best Yahweh!

Nothing created by the only Creator could ever surpass His glory, power, and truth because without Him—His power, nothing can be. It's like saying I can make a better man than the Great I Am, just give me a little dirt. I need some water, fire, food—I need. If you say I need and cannot create from your own source, you are not a creator but a manipulator of what's been created and put at your disposal!

The devil is not a creator he is only a manipulator, a corrupter, a liar, and a thief! He steals that which the Lord creates and claims it to be his. He is not able to create anything. The gifts of demons, fallen angels, are only in their possession because the Creator gave them to them.

> *"If you have a Need, you CAN'T best the LORD!"*

The devil was dumb to believe he could outdo, out create, or duplicate the most high; and us being mortal men, how much more are we deceived to believe our miniscule selves are capable of boxing with the Creator of the Universe! Laughable but boy do men try!

This inevitable fate of failure didn't shift nor scare satan, because his pride became great and over shadowed the light once in him! The Bible says the eye is the gate to your soul (Matthew

6:22). It is the entry point to your being. What you see, you can become. Protect your vision. Through your eyes you can bring in light and project the light within you. If that light were dark or bright, it will shine through your eyes.

The devil exposes himself by the actions his children make. Don't envy those that have given their lives over to the ecstasy, those who have settled for a counterfeit than the real McCoy. The devil and his kingdom are fighting a losing battle and anyone not under the covering of the Most High will be affected. Believers must cover their children because if they don't they are prime targets.

Our children are gateways the devil attempts to use to bring distraction, chaos, and trouble in our lives. Having children that depart from the Lord's ways because they weren't taught them, is a big problem in today's society. The parents say they don't teach their children about the Lord so not to stifle their decision making process. This is in direct opposition to what we are taught as believers!

We are taught, "Train up a child in the way he should go, And when he is old he will not depart from it (Proverbs 22:6." Surely, if they never knew the Lord, they will step away from Him. To the ones that taste the Lord they find He is good, worthy of your trust and blessings will befall them (Psalm 34:8).

Man can chase every ecstasy and never find a fitting substitute for having the Lord Almighty in their lives. If you raised them right and they are running, they will turn to the Lord, but if you have failed your children; pray, fast, and watch. The Lord is able to overcome any circumstance and make a way where there appears no way. We are taught not to give up nor doubt the power of the Almighty because our doubt can block progress!

"And this is the confidence that we have in Him, that, if we ask any thing according to His will, He heareth us (1 John 5:14)." Anything you ask in my Name will be given if you are in my will and don't doubt (Mark 11:23-24). Doubt cancels out your prayers!

We may try to fight the Word but it condemns us already if you don't believe (John 3:18). No one has to curse your life, if you don't believe or choose not to hear the voice of the Lord. If you are deaf to His Voice, will, your life is lived absent of Him. There is no greater punishment. The Lord is Love. He is the Creator of Life and the Source of unlimited Power!

"Doubt cancels out Prayer!"

You are a gadget disconnected from the power, you won't function and everything in your hand will not function according to His will for your life. Everything around you will die, age, become useless, close enough to touch, but never possible to have and keep. You can be so close you can touch progress but it remains out of your grasp because you are not in His line of sight, line of blessings.

You can attempt to box the Almighty and

protect your god. You see if the Lord doesn't sit on the throne in your life and you do, something else, or the devil, you are guilty of idolatry. The Lord is a jealous Spirit that will share His glory with no one—not even with you!

If you understand the boxing game, you would understand that boxing is just as much physical as it is mental—the same is true in the Spirit. The head leads the body and sends signals to have your body perform. The brain is also the piece that reasons and makes judgment calls for what's the next move. Reaction without contemplation is not going to be a fair battle, but a lost across the board.

The battle, the Bible says, begins in the mind. What you believe—not what you read, will determine your life's direction. It is not enough to only read the Bible, information, evidence, it needs to be believed so that it is set and established in your life.

If you believe in the Bible, you will do what it says. If you believe in yourself, you will do what you want. If you believe what others say about you, your condition, your future, you will live accordingly.

It's amazing how many people believe statements and ideas that are contrary to what the Bible says about them. The Truth, we choose to believe in a lie; then we are offended at the Lord when He exposes the flaws in our logic—in our gods. The Bible talks about the idols man worships that are dumb, mute, powerless, over worshiping the true and mighty I AM (Habakkuk 2:18-20)! The God that can move on our behalf is Holy and all-powerful, yet we give Him no respect. We instead attempt to spit upon His name, His Word, His ways and choose our filthy rags—the ecstasy.

When we attempt to box YHWH, we are putting our thoughts before His. We are taking man's thoughts over His and we believe that the Lord's thoughts are beneath us (Isaiah 58:8-9). The Bible says the opposite, so when we operate with this logic we are calling the Creator a liar.

The Bible tells the opposite, however, the Lord is not a man in which He will lie (Numbers 23:19). The Lord needs not to lie because what He speaks will come to past (Isaiah 55:11). How can you fight the Lord Almighty that has never LOST a battle?

He wins battles with and for His children that everyone is dumbfounded on how He won! Old testament wars was said once not to be studied at a college level because the wars should have never been won. How can a trumpet and shouting win a battle?

How can instruments cause the opposing team to kill themselves? The Hebrews sat upon the mountain and watched their enemy be struck with confusion and slaughter each other; and then they walked in and took their inheritance

"He wins wars with No Hands, Bullets, Knives but the Word!"

(2 Chronicles 20:21-23). No fight was required, but faith and belief in the Word of the Lord.

He told them they would win the battle, but they had to believe it! When you don't believe the Lord you are disobedient. You lean on your own understanding! The Bible says that obedience is greater than sacrifice (1 Samuel 15:22). The Lord doesn't care what you are willing to do, but He cares about what you believe, practice, because that is why you do what you do!

What is in you will come out to the light. You do not hide the Word under a lampshade, but you put it on a lampstand so the world can see it (Luke 11:33). If you read, watch, and listen to the things that are unholy, you are fighting a losing battle to believe you can acquire righteousness. Righteousness is not earned but imputed on His children by Him (Romans 4:3).

"Righteousness is not earned, but accredited to man by Yah!"

To get the gifts of the Lord you have to be given them, we can't steal from Yah. There are people, entities, businesses, governments, religions believing they can take what the Lord has made and give it to whom they desire. This will never be true; the Lord cannot fail, or loose (Acts 5:39). The thief will be tossed out (Matthew 22:13). His ways and understanding are beyond ours; the peace He gives surpasses all understanding (Philippians 4:7).

How can you fight what is beyond your understanding and expect to win? The fight is not in the flesh but in the Spirit and the Word is your power, your sword, and your defense against the tricks of the enemy. The ecstasy can be denied when the Word is your compass. Resist the devil and he will flee (James 4:7). Resisting the devil means speaking, believing, standing, and having faith in the Word!

The Word is who Yeshua is; He is the Word made into flesh sent to redeem man by being a perfect sacrifice (Hebrews 10:14). The Lord gave dominion of earth to man and man allowed the devil to trick him. The Lord gave us back our dominion through the Word, through His power, and sacrifice. The First Adam had man fall and the Second Adam redeem all that choose to receive the gift He brings.

Yeshua was sent to those seeking the Lord and those that do not want Him, not willing to give up their gods, do not deserve Him (Luke 14:26). If you do not desire Him then "yes" He did not die for you, but to those that believe. "Who is His mother, father, sister, or brother only those that do the will of the Father," says Matthew 12:50. We must not have this inclusive concept that all people are righteous, YHWH fearing, lovers of the Word, Truth, but there are vessels of honor and dishonor.

The Bible says there are vessels for honor and dishonor (Romans 9:21-22). Not everyone on the earth will accept the gift although all have access. There are children of the most high and children of the worker of iniquity. The battle should not be with the Lord, with the Word, but against the kingdom of darkness.

If you are not a believer than you are a non-believer. You either belong to the Kingdom of Light and Life, or the kingdom of death, destruction, lies, idolatry, lust, murder, hatred, and every wicked thing (Matthew 12:30). The Word has won the battle and took away the keys for hell, death, and the grave (Revelation 1:18).

> *"No one can pluck you out of the Lord's Hand!"*

> *"O death, where is your sting? O hades, where is your victory? The sting of death is sin, and the strength of sin is in the law. But thanks be to God, who gives us the victory through our Lord Yeshua the Christ."*

~ 1 Corinthians 15:55-57~

Death has no sting or victory thanks to Yeshua. There is protection in the hands of the Almighty. No devil can touch you nor pluck you out of His hand but you must abandon it (John 10:28-29).

When you feed into the ecstasy you walk out of the hands of Jehovah. Where the Lord is, there's protection, provision, joy, and peace; where He is not there is lawlessness and every wicked thing. So if you will fight, fight a battle already won. Fight for a worthy cause for your effort and time. The Lord is undefeated and He will remain so. He is not intimidated or fearful of losing any battle.

If you want to evade the trick and traps of the enemy, don't cave to the ecstasy. The devil is a liar that wants man to be were he is, in hell, damned and never able to receive grace, love, joy, and peace. The Word, Yeshua is the Prince of Peace (Isaiah 9:6), and the devil is the author of robbery, destruction, and lies (John 8:44). Don't let him choke out your promises, joy, peace, love, and the Word.

TRUST AND OPEN YOUR EYES

We can pretend with men, and strive with man, all of our days if we do not open our eyes to see the compassion in the Word. "To have compassion with no action is no compassion at all," Pastor W Michael Turner of Kingdom of God Ministries International, told me. The Lord gave and continues to give to demonstrate His compassion for humankind.

The trick of the enemy that is working in the world is to convince man that there is no battle in the spirit; and that only what is happening in this world matters. What matters is race, money, status, houses, cars, shoes—carnal things. The exact opposite is paramount to understand.

The ecstasy is the trick that convinces indulgers that sin is going to put you in a better place than those following the Word and will of the Great I Am. The high is soon fleeting, the fall is grand, and the destruction is vast with an ideal to be long standing. The devil doesn't just come for you but for your legacy! He wants to cut you off and every good thing that could happen to you and stop love from existing for you.

The devil is a liar and the truth isn't in him.

His promises come with a payoff that no man in his right mind would desire to pay. Fame, riches, houses, cars, people are not worth eternal separation from the Most High! Will you allow the ecstasy to separate you from the Love of the Creator?

Open your eyes and trust the Word when told the devil is not your friend but your accuser (1Timoty 4:13). When you cave to the ecstasy it is not the Lord that accuses you, but satan that reports your sin to the King. As if that is necessary.

"The devil is your accuser not your Friend!"

The devil is not worthy to be trusted and selling him your soul for any amount is not a good deal. All gifts from the devil come with regret, a catch, and are not given in good faith—the devil isn't capable. He lies, steals, and destroys everything he touches he manipulates.

His plan is to use you to destroy yourself, your potential, and those connected or that love you. People may wonder why folks, children, spouses, possibilities, love, joy, peace and the more walk out of their lives. The devil and doctrines of demons that you're holding on to, safeguarding, worshipping is choking the good out of your life.

Light and darkness cannot walk together, are not equally yoked, and they don't agree. Oil and water doesn't agree in nature same as light and darkness don't mix but they separate! The Lord separates His children from those that don't belong. If men don't open their eyes and subject themselves to the Lord, the Lord will take your children, wife, and give it to His son (Deuteronomy 28:30-31).

Yes the woman you maybe engaged to will marry another.

"Light and Darkness don't mix but Separate!"

The mother of your child or children will marry another and another man will raise your children. Tell me you haven't seen this curse operating in the world because of men that didn't heed the warning of the Lord? The Lord takes our obedience seriously and our choice to chase the ecstasy likewise.

The battles that are sent your way, the Lord is more than able and willing to fight! Consider the account of Elisha. Elisha was a faithful servant of the Lord and he was a man that could hear the Lord. The Lord gave him divine wisdom to know and understand the plans of the enemy's camp, warring with the Hebrews.

When Elisha got a Word he reported his findings to the nation and they were able to prepare for every attack and overcome their enemy. The king thought it was a mole in his camp and he sifted his army only to find Elisha was the culprit. Elisha was getting military strategies, private information from the Great I Am.

These men were so foolish. How could they think it possible to stop YHWH, the Creator of heaven and earth from speaking? Not possible. So their plans again were told to Elisha and he was waiting on them because he was confident in the

Lord's ability to protect him (2 Kings 6:15-20). His servant who had eyes wide shut, could not see and was panicking.

People around you cannot understand your peace, your confidence, unless the Lord almighty opens their eyes! The Word must quicken your spirit and open your eyes to know the Great I Am. Yeshua said truly the Lord has shown you who I am when Peter said He was the Christ (Matthew 16:16). The Word has to be given to you and the Spirit gives you understanding. To read the Bible means nothing without the Spirit (Mark 4:12).

You can forever hear but not understand, forever see but not perceive reads Mark 4:12. You can speak with no power. Information is not enough, you need the Holy Spirit living in you and you will become a vessel for honor. You must become a living sacrifice laying down your entire life to have your eyes open!

The Lord will not accept lukewarm, half stepping, and His love cast out all fear (1 John 4:18)! Elisha prayed to the Lord and asked Him to open the servant's eyes. The preacher is sent to give the Word so the lost may hear and receive salvation (Romans 10:14-15). The preacher is more than a speaker, they are mouthpieces used by the Lord to awaken His children from their slumber. The preacher is also expected to be the shepherd over the Lord's people, meaning they are responsible for the flock put in their care.

After the prayer of Elisha, the Lord granted his petition and opened the eyes of the servant

Gehazi. When his eyes were opened he saw like Elisha. He saw the angels, the chariots, and the army that was backing Elisha. He finally understood the confidence that was in Elisha. He knew what it was like to be fearless. He now knows how to stand in the face of giants and not flinch.

Has your eyes been open to see? Do you know how to trust the only good God? Allow Him to open your eyes and pour into you assuring you of your confidence. In 1 Peter 3:5 we are to be able at all times, in and out of season, in good and bad times, to give an account for why we believe in the Most High! We believe because our eyes have been opened. The ecstasy has no power over the Lord's children. Our lord has compassion on us and cast our sins into the depths of the sea (Micah 7:19).

To have your eyes opened is to know who you are. To know who you are is to acknowledge your power, your purpose, and walk in your divine calling. Your eyes are wide shut if you walk in fear, defeat, doubt, and religion. Religion did not redeem or save you! The Word that is Yeshua did. Open your ears and hear what the Lord is saying to His children!

"You are a Peculiar People, a Royal Priesthood!"

You are a peculiar people a royal priesthood and are to be ye separated (1 Peter 2:9). We must be separate and in order to be as such, our perception and viewpoint must be connected to the Word. You will see the world, your problems, and choices differently when your ears are opened. If you walk in the darkness you will stumble and fall, but with the light you can see (Proverbs 4:19).

If two are blind walking together wont they both fall in a ditch (Matthew 15:14)? Yes they will, we have to open our eyes and not follow blind guides. What does it mean to open your eyes? It means to open your life, mind, being, and spirit to the Word and purpose of the Kingdom of Yah. The Lord is here and He said to seek Him while He still maybe found (Isaiah 55:6).

Open your eyes to the leadership around you, to the vessels used for honoring Him. Don't listen to blind guides that lead you to sin no matter if they are in our outside of the church. The devil has wolves in sheep clothing everywhere (Matthew 7:15). No man will have an excuse for why he settled for religion instead of knowing Christ.

The Bible says, Christ at Final Judgment will tell you, religion practitioners, get away from me you worker of iniquity for I never knew you (Luke 13:27). "Knew you" is an intimate way of knowing a person. It is not a distant learning but a strong bond like marriage the Lord desires with us.

To say you are married and not know your husband/wife is to not be married. How then can we expect to convince ourselves or others that we are believers, if we are not married or a bondservant of Christ? We must examine ourselves and see if we are in the faith (2 Corinthians 13:5). You cannot practice lawlessness and say you are in right standing with the Lord.

When your eyes are shut you will see no problem with your sin. You will be comfortable living in iniquity and what may appear to be common sense is not common. Sin desensitizes us to reality. Consider the music, movies, TV shows, and entertainment men and women engage in.

How many of those films encourage us to live alternative lifestyles? How many songs must we listen to that degrade men or women and bring them lower than their divine Creator intended? Our television shows make intimacy to be nothing more than freestyle sex, unattached to the love and covenant the Lord ordained.

> *"Sin desensitizes us to reality!"*

The audience is serenade by this generation of entertainment—ecstasy and the world's attempt to bring these ungodly ideals into the church. As such, the lives of the Lord's children are warped because our lifestyles, homes, marriages, and frame of thought change. Entertainment is a form of programming. Whatever your eye, ear, and mouth engage in will help to shape your choices.

The Bible says to flee from the thought or presence of evil (1 Thessalonians 5:22). That means programming, music, entertainment, and all relative forms that would cause you to sin we ought to refrain from. Many may be sadden to find they have to fast forward, skip scenes in movies or stop watching many films all together; because the film is entertaining spirits they don't want active in their members. Horror movies are one of the sneakiest kinds of films that open the floodgates for spirits to invade a viewer's frame of mind.

Brings to mind the story of the man that lived according to the 10 commandments but would not give up his richest to serve the Lord (Matthew 19:19-22). Is there an ecstasy you are chasing, false securities you are not willing to give away, or other things you love that keep you away from the promise? Some refuse to give up food, entertainment, people, thoughts, or ideals. If we walk with our eyes wide shut we will fail and it is only a matter of how long will we continue to stumble in the dark.

The longer we slow down the process to open our eyes and ears the longer we will walk in darkness. To open your eyes one must hear the Word of the Lord and to hear you must have a preacher. The preachers are called to the sick, broken hearted, lonely, abandoned and hurting. Yeshua said the Word came for those in need and not those claiming to be whole without Him (Mark 2:17). For people believing they don't need the Word, Love, the presence of the Most High in their life, surely their eyes and ears are closed.

"Christ came for the sick, not those convinced they don't need Him!"

When your eyes and ears are open, the Holy Spirit connects with your spirit and leads you to truth. "But ye have a unction from the Holy One, and ye know all things," says 1 John 2:20; His children must be diligent and trained to hear the voice of the Lord. The Holy One of the Old Testament is the same today as of Old, which simple means He still speaks today!

> *"The Lord is active. He didn't set it and forget it!"*

Many are tempted to believe the world was created and set on a course to carry on with the daily happens absent of the Lord's influence. This way of thought couldn't be more far from the truth. The Lord is sovereign, omnipotent, omnipresent, and omniscient. The Lord is the Great Creator because of His ability to not be a respecter of time or person, to shape the world and all its inhabitants to conform to His will—then still uphold His word of free will!

The Lord in His infinite wisdom created man and everything. He gave them one command, "Don't eat from this tree of knowledge (Genesis 2:17)." They were free to do whatever they chose, even if it was in objection to the Lord's command. Yahweh gave man everything they needed to survive and topped it off by given him dominion over the land. These perfect beings, gave ear to the devil who talked Adam into jepordizing his dominion in exchange for what they thought was a superior wisdom.

Adam and Eve made this choice, gambling on what the Lord promised for a chance of what the serpent had to offer. They gave up their dominion in exchange for a prize that was not worth the price. What they got was death, destruction, despair, pain, hurt, and everything the serpent brings.

They were not blessed as the Lord had blessed, but were cursed because they chased the ecstasy. Adam and Eve desired to be like the Creator and ended up being shut away from Him because of their disobedience. The devil's aim is not to open your eyes, but to close them!

> *"The devil wants to eternally separate you from the Lord!"*

Entertainment, music, song, dance, drugs, people, attitudes, and feelings can all be used by the devil to close your eyes, heart, mind, and soul to the Lord. When you embrace the ecstasy (sin) through these channels, you turn your back on the Word.

You exchange your allegiance from the blessing and promises given to man by Yahweh for the ecstasy and accept the disappointment that the devil offers. The devil brings the curse, hurt, pain, disease, and death. "Then when lust (ecstasy) hath conceived, it bringeth forth sin: and sin, when it is finished, bringeth forth death (James 1:15)." Who or what do you serve?

HOLY SPIRIT REVELATION: SERVE

Yeshua said the greatest among men are not those that demand to be served but those that willfully choose to serve (Matthew 23:11-12). We are all bondservants of the true King if we believe. This is not manmade slavery, where abuse, manipulation, persecution, and torment occupy. Many may read the Bible and conclude that Yahweh authored slavery, no He authorized decency and order; nothing about manmade slavery can comply.

The Lord condones freewill and the idea of manmade slavery is in direct opposition to the concept of freedom. As a bondservant you are not of your own, because you follow the Most High and commit to Him your life. This is a godly appointed servitude and nothing like the manmade, devil counterfeit.

"The Lord is the God of decency and order!"

Slavery through history is the process of one being owned by another. This slave owner does not have to follow a strict set of values, protocol, or requirements for how they treat their slave. There is no law to what you can or cannot do to a slave according to man because the slave is viewed as nothing more than property. If you are property, like an animal, a dog sent to obey your owner's wishes, many feel you have no rights.

Ironically, the same people that thought it fine to treat humans any kind of way are the same ones that would fight for animal rights. Case in point, people support abortion but are against putting your dogs—your property to sleep, having them live outside, and being tied up to a chain. The dogcatchers euthanize animals at will, but if you do it, it is animal cruelty.

We support people boxing and fighting to the death throughout history, but if chickens or dogs fight you need to serve time. Ludicrous! I don't support these matches, but in history, people have done worse with no consequence.

This same group complains about how many dogs are on the streets, encourage you to adopt, but then want to dictate how you provide, shelter, and feed them. Animals were treated way better than people if you take a peek at history or modern day laws.

"All life Matters, born or forming, regardless of race!"

The Bible never condoned how man manipulated bondservant, handmaiden to mean man's definition of slavery as was played out in history and is today. Servitude has always been a useful practice to learn a skill. Indentured servants were common in times past and many people of today are finding that a trade certificate can be just as profitable as a degree. So why do many conclude being a bondservant is of the devil?

A sincere bondservant has to be within the scope of what the Most High created, which would be according to His Word. The Greek word doulos has been translated to read slave, bondservant, or servant in Bibles. The definition of doulos, "one who is subservient to, and entirely at the disposal of, his master; a slave," cannot be as plainly understood as lead on.

This servant is unlike a slave because the servant makes the choice to voluntarily serve another according to agreeable terms. If you make a choice to be at the disposal of someone, you are not a slave according to societal norms. You have a job!

Slavery in modern society is not chosen but forced upon unwilling subjects that are beaten, threaten, or coerced into submission. Slavery involving blacks around the world never appeared to be voluntary servitude; neither are the women and men of many nations that are sex trafficked offering to serve their masters happily. Torment, fear, coercion, family sacrifice is more often the reason for said service and false loyalty.

Although the Lord could force all human nature to serve Him that is not His will. He makes an appeal to man through a preacher, as it is written:

"How then can they call on the One they

have not believed in? And how can they hear without someone to preach? And how can they preach unless they are sent?

~Romans 10:14-15~

To be a servant of the Most High is an honor and to walk in victory or struggle for Christ is consider a reward among believers (Romans 8:17). Seems like a senseless solution at first thought but consider this. If you were a life long admirer of the justice system, you watched court shows, you read books, you have ambitions to go to college some day if money lines up. One day you encounter Judge Awesome live and in person.

You two have a great conversation and he extends a offer for him to train you. He helps you get into the right school, coach you to insure you pass your classes, get you through the bar, endorse you for creditability, and he will help you find a job!

"To serve the Lord by being His mouthpiece is no petty service!"

Many of us would say in an instant, where do I sign up to have those kinds of guarantees? He says I simple need you to listen, trust, and follow my instructions. We have to study and meet everyday; you also have to follow my instructions carefully.

I will advise you on what relationships need

to end and will ask you to change personality traits that would cause you to struggle or fail. I will be here to help you no matter the problem. My only request of you in return is that you help others like I help you! Simply, refer them to me.

Is this not what Christ does for those that believe? Does He not ask that we follow the Word, be careful not to sin, and give up on lifestyle choices that would cause immediate or long-term harm? But how simple it is for many to yield their being to be a vessel of dishonor instead of honor (2 Timothy 2:20)? Many would choose to serve a senseless god, a system that is unjust, and follow a social order that is impractical, wicked at its core.

If a man gave us this opportunity we would jump on it and call ones who didn't a fool. Yet day after day we choose not to be a bondservant of Christ, but a joint heir with satan. How so? To be a bondservant of Christ is to be yoked, walking together with Christ. You have made up your mind that you are going to serve Christ and Him alone. You determine that His ways are better than yours in spite of the adversity before you.

If you look at the voluntary servants of Christ their roads weren't rosy every day. Some were shipwrecked, jailed, stoned, put in a fiery furnace, dropped in a den of hungry lions, hung, beheaded, laughed at, censored, mocked, and much more that's not listed. So why serve Christ even unto the point of death, rejection by your family, friends, peers, and/or society? To choose to deny the ecstasy of life, surely the gift has to be greater than the fruit of sin.

The gift is eternal life, peace, joy and favors in this life and the one to come. When we walk with Christ we have an internal compass that leads our steps and we know not the end, but trust the Lord's hand (Psalm 23). The Lord says, "He will never leave us nor forsake us" but will be with us through our good times, life lessons, even until the end of this age (Hebrews 13:5).

The Lord is committed to every indentured servant, bondservant, and child of His looking like Christ when His work is completed (Philippians 1:6). The characteristics of Christ is compassion, peace, healing, friend, power, strength, confidence, boldness, wisdom, charity, freedom, loyalty, sacrifice, and too much to list. Would you like for when people talk about you to mention descriptions like these? Yet we run from serving Christ, whose intention is to show you how to be like Him so you too can reap the benefits.

Everything worth having in life cost you something, even the Bible says to count up the cost for any action (Luke 14:28). Salvation is free but it cost your life! To be a bondservant, child of the Most High, you have to voluntarily subject your will to the will of the Lord. You have to allow the Lord to be your Master, instructor, teacher, guide, and Father.

The Lord requires your all and to offer less than that will not satisfy Him. The

"Salvation is free, BUT cost your Life!"

Lord hates when we are undecided, lukewarm. Lukewarm is not hot or cold, salt or fresh; it's talking about the Word but not believing in its power. Consider the parable about the sower in Matthew 13:4-8.

> *"And when he sowed, some seeds fell by the way side, and the fowls came and devoured them up: Some fell upon stony places, where they had not much earth: and forthwith they sprung up, because they had no deepness of earth: And when the sun was up, they were scorched: and because they had no root, they withered away. And some fell among thorns; and the thorns sprung up, and choked them: But others fell into good ground, brought forth fruit, some a hundredfold, some sixtyfold, some thirtyfold."*

You have a seed, the Word, but what you do with it varies like this parable outlines. Did you believe it, bury it into your heart, and practice through life application—establishing strong roots deep into the ground? Or is the latter true, the birds take it away, its chocked out by the thorns, and the fire burns it up?

When you chase the ecstasy the fire of sin consumes the seed (Word). No life can grow from a seed not properly planted and nurtured. Plants don't grow by leaving the seed in its package, but by planting, nurturing, caring, and providing an atmosphere for it to thrive.

If you don't give the Word an atmosphere to produce, you will lack the power of it. If you don't have the power but just know the verse when you encounter demons in high places, they will tell you, "Yeshua we know, Paul we know, but who are you (Acts 19:15)?" Knowing the Word, but denying the power will get you nowhere.

To operate with the appearance of godliness and deny the power is not beneficial to anyone (2 Timothy 3:5). Because of Christ we are able to pull down strongholds, cast out demons, set captives free, give hope to the hopeless, be a parent to an orphan, and a help meet to the widow and the poor. When we forsake Christ, we turn away from every good thing He brings into our life. No good thing will the Lord keep from those who walk uprightly (Psalm 84:11).

There are benefits to following Christ same as there are consequences for those chasing the ecstasy. The Lord's gifts add no sorrow unlike satan's gifts (Proverbs 10:22). The devil tempted Christ in the garden to sin, chase His desires over the Father's.

Yes, Christ too is a bondservant to the Father, so he expects us to do the same. Christ is the Word of the Father made into flesh (John 1:1). Our words do what we tell them to, but if your words could speak, had flesh, would they choose to serve you or expose your inner thoughts, heart?

What example would Christ have been if He would choose not to voluntarily lay His life, power, authority down in observation of the Father's will? Christ yielding His power to the Father demonstrates His acknowledgement that the Father is greater. Do we not entrust our lives willingly to those we trust can care for us? But not everyone we trust is out for our good. Some people, entities, ideologies, spirits lead us to death and not life.

The ecstasy wants you to be a slave, addict, addicted to a substance that kills you and not set you free. Christ wants you free to serve Him and others. We can only serve one master, be fresh or salty, clean or unclean, righteous or unrighteous, a vessel of honor or dishonor.

When the Bible says The Lord loves a cheerful giver that is not limited to money. Being a cheerful giver of your time, energy, thoughts, ideas, lifestyle, will, money is all a part of what the Lord requires. To harp only on money limits many to think paying money cheerfully only pleases the Almighty. No, Isaiah 55:1 says,

"Ho! Everyone who thirsts, Come to the waters; And you who have no money, Come, buy and eat. Yes, come, buy wine and milk without money and without price.

Where else can you buy, eat and drink with no money? How can that be possible unless you are not buying into a cash or worldly system but a different one with a special currency? Faith is the currency of heaven because without faith it is impossible to please The Lord (Hebrews 11:6). The Lord doesn't care about how much you give or keep from the offering; He cares about your heart and why you give.

Giving should be out of worship and done with a cheerful heart to serve not out of compulsion (2 Corinthians 9:7). It's wrong to guilt trip people into giving and man should realize giving grandly doesn't move YHWH. Giving grandly doesn't even move us in the natural.

If you felt taken, used, abused, you aren't going to keep giving willfully; but if you believe and feel a part of a solution nothing will hold you back. The cheerful giver holds nothing back because they are sold-out on the cause, the promise.

"Giving is a form of worship, service, and agreement to a cause!"

The Lord will be indebted to no man and any that gives to Him, to the poor, He will repay (Proverbs 19:17). Christ further said,

> *"Verily I say unto you, There is no man that hath left house, or brethren, or sisters, or father, or mother, or wife, or children, or lands, for my sake, and the Gospel's, but he shall receive an hundredfold now in this time, houses, and*

brethren, and sisters, and mothers, and children, and lands, with persecutions; and in the world to come eternal life."

~Mark 10:29-30~

Every servant of Christ has a promise that the Lord will bless him/her a hundred-time fold for His namesake. This covering, protection, love is unlike a worldly slave agreement. The world's form of slavery seeks to steal from you, take your resources to fulfill their needs, wants, desires with no care of your wellbeing.

Bondservants of Christ receive promises, love, protection, covering, and He cares for your wellbeing. Compassion with no action is not caring at all but simply recognizing the obvious. The Lord recognized our needs and was moved to give to provide for us

The true living YHWH is unlike any Greek or false idle god.

"The Lord only has Children He Loves!"

He lives, breathes, redeems, cares, and has the ability—the will to make changes in your life. He is the only that will be with you no matter the highs or lows you experience. Unlike our friends, jobs, relationships that give up on us once we are unable to perform, fulfill a need, or service.

It was while we were still sinners, acting in opposition to Yahweh, He gave His Son to redeem us to demonstrate His undying LOVE. He sticks with us closer than any brother (Proverbs 18:24). The Most High exhibits agape love toward his servants, children. The devil has no friends but lots of children. The Lord only has children He loves!

EXAMINE YOURSELF

To know if you are a child of the Most High, you must examine yourself to see if you are in fact in the faith (2 Corinthians 13:5). We are cautioned that everyone that calls the Lord, Lord is not going to heaven, does not believe, and are not born again believers (Matthew 7:21)! What a great trick the devil plays on man to have us think because we do good works, sing songs, read our Bible on occasion that we are doing Adonia a favor.

We are instructed that those that do good to and for others do themselves a great service, but as to the Creator not necessarily so much. If you pay off your debts, respect your elders, obey road signs, treat your spouse well, wouldn't that make all things go well for you? You would have no debt. Others would respect you because you respect them. Your spouse would love you because you show and demonstrate love to them. That would mean what you do for others would likely turn back to you.

There are rules of nature and then there is the supernatural. Nature works according to the natural order. As long as you operate in the natural order many things you desire and work for may come to you, not because Yah sent them but because you worked for them. You can make things happen in your life. The Lord gave power to all creation to make a choice for what direction our lives take and who we will serve.

People who chose to make wise decisions will reap the results as is laid out in Proverbs. The Bible says His people perish from a lack of wisdom (Hosea 4:6). So those that have the wisdom and operate in it are those that benefit regardless of servitude.

"There are rules of nature and then there is the supernatural!"

So what's the benefit of being a child of I AM and say a child that chases the ecstasy, their own lust? For those that chase their own high, their success and future relies solely on their ability to maintain what they accomplish. The natural order, it rains on the just and the unjust (Matthew 5:45). Simply put, all people will have good and bad days because rain shows no partiality to man.

Those that have their footing in their own ability when they are unable to perform, loose it all. If you are an entrepreneur who built your company from scratch everything succeeds or fails based on you. You lead the sales team, all departments report to you, and you trust no one as your number two. You are numero uno and besides you there is no figurehead for your company.

What happens when you grow ill? Your spouse leaves you and your children abandoned you? Your friends want nothing to do with you or you loose your sound mind? Does it not affect everything you built?

Although man likes to think we can function like a robot with no emotion, no hindrances, we find that to be far from the truth. If your personal life is in disarray the rest of your life is affected. Some resort to substances to numb the pain or to forget, but that is only a temporary fix. The problem, situation, rain is still their. The life you created you are watching wash away with the rain. Many who see their entire life savings, family, lifestyle washed away with a market crash commit suicide; resort to drinking, drugs and even fall into a medicated depression.

What happens when Kingdom kids are dealt a bad hand? Their spouse leaves them, their children are taken, jobs disappear, health dwindles, and their life looks like a storm is hovering above. They turn to their Father in Heaven and give Him praise. They seek His face for direction and answers for next steps. Do they hurt? Yes they do, but they draw strength from their Source.

Your source is your lifeline and if the source is you, you cannot afford a down day. The world continues to turn because Adonia set it in motion at the beginning of time and it will do what He said until He says otherwise. Will your body continue to move for as long as your voice tells it to? Will your heart keep pumping for

"Is your Source, indestructible, omnipotent, omniscient, sovereign?"

as long as your mind thinks it to? When the source of your strength is indestructible, omnipotent, omniscient, and sovereign there is nothing that may happen that will shake your foundation.

Believers have their foundation in the Word of the Lord. They do not live on bread alone but from every Word from the Lord (Matthew 4:4). If you examine your life, who or what is your source of influence? If the Word is your influence then it is as the Bible says, "If you love me, keep my commandments (John 14:15)." The Lord's children love the Word (Christ) and are not out chasing the ecstasy but serving the Lord.

Servants of the Lord are not servants during just the good season, the blessing, but are serving in spite of what conditions that may come. Job, a servant of the Most High lacked nothing at one point in his life. He was blessed with children, had a lovely wife, owned property, and took care of his servants. Yet, the devil accused him of only serving the Lord because He gave him everything.

The Lord called the devil a bluff and bragged all the more on Job. The devil thought that Job would curse "YHWH" and die if the Lord took his riches, children, and turned his wife against him. Job lost a child one by one—tragically, his wife told him to curse Yah and die. His friends, who came ideally to comfort him, judged, condemned, and accused him of bringing this on himself.

He attempted to defend himself first to his friends to no avail and then appealed to Adonia to grant him death. He asked the Lord why his life had gone in the direction it had? The Lord was silent to his petition until He decided to answer.

When the Lord opened His Mouth to speak to Job, He asked who are you to question my choice? Who is any man that he thinks to counsel YHWH? *"What man knows the Mind of YHWH and is His counsel?"* Romans 11:34 reads, "Who has known the mind of the Lord? Or who has been His counselor?"

Job repented and the Lord told him to pray for his friends. After, the Lord blessed Job all the more because He chose that it pleased Him to see Job blessed. When you serve the Lord, it does not mean everything will go your way or that He will teach you life lessons only through the lives of others. Job, innocent, still had a lesson to learn in this scenario. Many believers struggle not because the Lord does not like them, they have sinned, but because there is a lesson to be learned and His glory to be had.

When we examine our life and see that our lives are not our own, but the Lord's, we give the Father the ability to decided what journey He sees fit for us. The Lord will not allow us to be tempted more than we can bear (1 Corinthians 10:13). It is always His mindset to have us line up, conform, and live out the Word. Defeat is not the Lord's gift to His children contrary to what some may like for believers to think.

We've talked about the natural realm, but

what about the supernatural? What gifts are there for believers in that realm? The spirit realm is where the Lord resides because He is Spirit (John 4:24). The Lord expects for His children to pray in spirit and in truth.

The natural world does not move Yah, but the spirit realm does. Believers are to walk by faith and not by sight (2 Corinthians 5:7). The spirit realm needs to be more real to us than the natural because the spirit leads the natural realm.

Take for example the account of Gideon. He was told that he would have the victory in battle against the Midianites. He too didn't have to pick up one sword or weapon—nor have a army large in company. The Lord in Judges 7 told him to select the men who lapped to drink and take those 300 with him. The others were sent home.

The Lord told Gideon, if he was scared to take Purah, and his servant told him of his dream. The dream foretold how Gideon would approach their tent and it would topple over. He was encouraged and listened to the voice of the Lord and this was a battle won by sounding a trumpet and breaking glass.

The Lord granted Elisha's request and opened the eyes of his servant to see the preparation Yah already made to protect them; He did the same for Gideon. That vision for him shut off every fearful thought. Truly, his life could have never been the same after witnessing a powerful demonstration of the Lord's presence in the earth in winning a battle never faught!

When you are not busy chasing the ecstasy you are focused on reading, studying, worshiping, and examining your life in light of the Word. The ecstasy is meant to kill your interest in the spirit realm because as long as you operate in the natural realm you can be stopped. Bodies are finite, jobs, people, dreams, resources in the hands of man. No man is infallible, but all fall short of the glory of Yahweh (Romans 3:23)!

What happens when you tap into the Spirit, when the Most High is your Source? You are unstoppable; you are more than a conqueror (Romans 8:37)! The Bible tells us that the Lord gives us power to pull down strongholds (2 Corinthians 10:4), demons in high places (Ephesians 6:2), and tread over serpents (Luke 10:19). This power is not subject to the natural but operating in the supernatural!

> *"Operating in the Spirit removes boundaries, working in the natural puts on the limits!"*

If you are addicted to the ecstasy you may be unaware of the battle happening in the spirit. The battle to take your soul and condemn you to hell, eternal separation from Yahweh, is more real than the streets you walk on. With a plate shift, a Word from YHWH, the earth can open up and swallow subjects in an instant (Numbers 26:10)!

The devil does not control Yahweh nor does the natural realm conform the Creator. The lord is able to operate on a plane where no one is His equal. His greatest foe, the devil, is His footstool! What can the world do to the believers except what the Lord allows? If the Lord is for you, who can be against you (Romans 8:31)?

> *"Awake, awake, put on strength, O arm of the Lord; Awake as in the days of old, the generations of long ago. Was it not you who cut Rahab in pieces, who pierced the dragon."*

~Isaiah 51:9~

The call to examine ourselves as described in 1 John is for believers to take inventory of their walk with Christ. We must not be lazy, an idle mind is the devil's workshop (Philippians 4:8) and so are idle hands (Proverbs 16:27-29).
We must keep our mind set on meditating on the Word day and night (Psalm 1:2).

In such meditation you are keeping the Word in your heart, mind, eye-gate so that you will not sin against the Lord (Joshua 1:8). If you don't know the Word you are the devils puppet. You have given yourself over to the ecstasy that has no reward outside of death.

Sin only leads to death and can not bring you life or anything truth

"The devil is a liar and no Truth is in him; so no Truth can he give!"

(Romans 6:23). True happiness, true love, joy, or peace the devil cannot give because he is a liar and the truth is not in him (John 8:44). How can the devil give you something he does not possess?

Yes, he can give you things, a wife, a job, a house, fame, and fortune but at what cost? Your servitude and soul is what he is after. He doesn't fight so much to have your soul but to keep you from given it to the Lord! By default, you go where he lives, hell. 2 Corinthians 13:5 says,

> *"Examine yourselves as to whether you are in the faith. Test yourselves. Do you not know yourselves, that Yeshua the Christ is in you?— unless indeed you are disqualified."*

Some translations read reprobate instead of disqualified. A reprobate mind is a common saying in the church, the meaning, lacking sound wisdom. Nebuchadnezzar was cursed with a reprobate mind, and ate grass as a punishment by Yahweh (Daniel 3, 4).

The Lord moves in the natural and touches those He chooses. He uses men to be vessels of special use or common (2 Timothy 2:20). Examine your walk; are you a vessel of gold and silver, or wood and clay? Choose this day, who you will serve.

YOU'RE NOT HOPELESS

You're not hopeless nor are you left without a comforter (John 14:18). My mercy and grace is sufficient for all your needs. When you accept sin, live in it—iniquity, you are saying the Word is not enough. The implication that the saving blood of Christ is not enough to redeem you is also implied. The Word says He will complete a work He started in you and that His mercy is sufficient for all your needs (Philippians 1:6, 2 Corinthians 12:9). If you fall, don't stay in a fallen state. Once you have been redeemed, don't allow the devil to call unclean what the Lord has cleansed (Acts 11:9). No matter what you did.

It may be tempting to think we are hopeless because we are born into sin and shaped in iniquity (Psalm 51:5). The truth is the opposite! From the Old to the New Testament the Lord provides a way of escape to His children. Moses, a mighty man of the Lord, was born at an incredible time. A time where Hebrew boys were to be killed on sight because the Pharaoh feared the population growth of the Hebrews.

The midwives would not kill the babies because they feared the Lord more than Pharaoh. The mother of Moses by faith hid her baby 3 months because she saw that he was beautiful; before she set him adrift in the Nile River (Hebrews 11:23). Pharaoh's daughter spotted this baby when she was bathing in the Nile and brought the baby home. The Pharaoh gave her permission to adopt him, and then she sent for his mother to nurse him for her!

Like Abraham, Moses' parents were asked to give their son to the Lord, but instead of Him taking their life, He protected it. He provided a ram for Abraham

"Give your Children to God and He will give them Back to You!"

and He allowed an Egyptian to adopt Moses. This adoption not only saved his life, but also gave him back to his parents to be raised. Moses did not grow up absent of the fact he was a Hebrew; he knew who and where he came from.

Not only was Moses special because the Lord picked him, he also suffered with physical disabilities, specifically in speech. Amazing the Lord never considered Moses stutter as a problem but he did. In life wont we give excuses for why we can't serve the Lord? We can't serve the Lord because of our past. We can serve the Lord because of our physical or mental handicap. The Lord doesn't always choose to remove the facts about you that man calls a handicap.

Paul had a thorn in his side that he prayed three times to be removed. His prayer was heard and the Lord provided him with an answer, "My grace is sufficient." Moses too had grace sufficient to allow him to fulfill the Lord's plan for his life. The Lord allowed him to use Aaron as his mouthpiece, but was very clear that Moses is His choice not Aaron (Exodus 4:14-17).

The excuse that Moses had was removed so that he could serve Yah and yes it was not in a way he expected; but the way the Lord provided. The Lord knows how to make away in a hopeless situation. Moses as he grew longed to help his nation and one day he took a life of an Egyptian to defend a Hebrew man. He thought no one had seen him, but soon he found enough people did see. He fled the country and went into the desert where he would meet his wife, and Ethiopian.

In our lives we have all made choices to serve our desires? Picking the wrong mate, cheating on our taxes, stealing from people or stores, fighting someone with words or in body. The Bible tells us all have fallen short of the glory of YHWH so we are all in need of salvation. We all need to repent and ask for forgiveness from the Lord.

Our Father is faithful to restore our hope and redeem our being. He will not leave us without a comforter and so His Spirit, Word (His Son) is also with us. Moses needed to know that the Great I Am would be with him when he went to the He-

"If you have an excuse, the Lord has an answer to eliminate it!"

brews. He desired to be fully convinced he was not alone, and he asked who do I say sent me? By what authority should they believe in what Aaron and I have come to say? The Lord said, "Tell them I Am sent you (Exodus 3:14)."

Even though he had a mouthpiece to speak for him, had a Word from the Lord, he still wanted more. So the Lord gave him a staff that had power to accomplish parting the waters, turning into a snake, and turning water into blood. Moses lacked nothing to fulfill his mission and he heard the Lord talk from a burning bush before all of this!

We are not much different from Moses. We want evidence, confirmation, and assurance that the Lord is with us. The Lord has given you His Son, His Word, the fellowship of the church and the Holy Spirit to affirm and assure you! We are not hopeless no matter the circumstance. You may have made a decision that has you in a physical or mental prison, guilty of murder, regret, hurt, and shame; but the Lord is able and willing to restore you.

"We want proof, assurance, evidence that the Lord is and He Provides!"

Moses was used to liberate the Hebrew nation from the grip of the Egyptian Pharaoh. That plan was on his life when he was born, set adrift on the Nile, when he became a murder, and as he grew older. We are all appointed before we are born to perform a certain job like Jeremiah was appointed to be a prophet, Moses to lead the Hebrews out of Egypt.

Paul, previously known as Saul was a persecutor of the Church of Christ. He killed Hebrews that acknowledge and accepted the Gospel of Christ. He wanted to see them rid out of the land and he personally was in the army to see to it. Paul grew up as a Pharisee and so he was familiar with the Torah. He was not persuaded to believe in Christ during his lifetime but after He visited him on the Damascus road.
Yeshua asked Paul in Acts 9:4-5,

> *"Saul, Saul, why do you persecute me? And he said who are you Lord? And He said, I am Yeshua whom you persecute: it is hard for (you) to kick against the pricks."*

Paul learned that day the voice of the Lord and received his first set of directions from Christ. He was told to go into the city and await further instructions but he was also struck blind. This simple command to go into the city was not so simple. Paul had to learn to trust in the Lord and now is the best time, when his senses had failed him.

Paul studied and grew in the faith. He was appointed an apostle beyond the 11th hour and he was humbled that the Lord sought a place for him given his history and timing. Not only did Christ call a murder—no less a murdered of His people to serve Him, but also to carry the Gospel to the

Gentiles.

Paul brought forth the message that both Israelites and Gentiles are joint heirs with Christ. He became a servant of the Gospel by the gift of Adonia's grace given him through the working of The Lord's power (Ephesians 3:1-11). He further says,

> *"Although I am less than the least of all Yawhew's people, this grace was given me: to preach to the gentiles the unsearchable riches of Christ, and to make plain to everyone the administration of this mystery."*

Paul considered himself the least of the apostles yet the Lord used him in a mighty way for the New Testament. Paul's life was a continual billboard of the Lord's grace and constant reminder the Lord can save and use whomever He desires. Paul had to confront and rebuke Peter about placing more on gentiles than the Lord desired.

"Those that are forgiven much LOVE Much!"

Paul understood that the Lord had forgiven him of much and likewise he wanted to give much (Luke 7:47). The lady forgiven of adultery in the account of Luke had the same gratefulness that Paul had towards the Lord. She understood that her sin was big, but do we see that our sins are big too? The reciprocal to forgiven much love much is also true, those who are forgiven little love or give little.

There is no such thing as a little sin, all sin is the same and there is no partiality to it (1 John 5:17). If you break one aspect of the law you are guilty of breaking it all (James 2:10). Why is the law so important? The Ten Commandments handed to Moses by the Lord are important because they establish the Most High's standard for human nature. The Lord created an expectation for all man to follow and it is by this standard we are all judged.

If you break one of the Ten Commandments you are guilty of breaking it all and the Bible says we all are guilty. If we say we have not sin, we are a liar and we accuse Yah of being a liar, and His Word is not in us (1 John 1:10). This may appear to be a hopeless situation but through Christ, Yahweh brought hope to the world!

Yeshua was born of the Spirit, unlike the first Adam born of the flesh (1 Corinthians 15:45). His father was not Joseph but the Holy Spirit, and as such, "Flesh is born of flesh, but Spirit is born of the Spirit (John 3:6)." Yeshua was not a mere man but the Lord with us, Emmanuel. The life of Christ had to be without sin so that He could be the perfect sacrifice that redeems all humanity.

"It was a perfect sacrifice by a perfect person to perfect some very imperfect peo-

ple. By that single offering, He did everything that needed to be done for everyone who takes part in the purifying process."

"The Holy Spirit confirms this: This new plan I'm making with Israel isn't going to be written on paper, isn't going to be chiseled in stone; This time I'm writing out the plan in them, carving it on the lining of their hearts."

"He concludes, I'll forever wipe the slate clean of their sins. Once sins are taken care of for good, there's no longer any need to offer sacrifices for them. So, friends, we can now – without hesitation walk right up to Yahweh, into "the Holy Place." Yeshua has cleared the way by the blood of His sacrifice, acting as our priest before Yahwheh. The Curtain into the Creator's presence is His body."

"So let's do it – full of belief, confident that we're presentable inside and out. Let's keep a firm grip on the promises that keep us going. He always keeps His word. Let's see how inventive we can be

in encouraging love and helping out."

~Hebrews 10:14-24 MSG~

We have the Ten Commandments that were previously engraved in stone that are now promised to be etched on our hearts. The veil that separated man from entering into the "Holies of Holies" in the temple is now removed at the cross. We can boldly approach the throne of grace and speak with the Father because the blood of Christ washes away our sins no matter how big! Christ is that important, His blood is that pure, and now it is up to us to choose to walk in His promise.

Will you choose to walk in the promises that Christ has provided to you or will you hide from the healing gift of Christ? Will you allow the devil to trick you that your sins are too large? The ecstasy of indulging in sin is more enjoyable—fun than following Christ! Will you allow him to trick you into believing a certificate is enough to profess your faith!

Don't be deceived by the tricks of religion. Religion did not die on the cross

"Heaven or Hell? This earth is not an Option!"

to redeem you, Yeshua, the Christ did! Through Him and only through Him are men redeemed. Great works you perform if not done out of love and worship for the Lord is simply you being a nice person. This is not enough to establish your place in eternal life. The spirit has a resting place, heaven or hell; this earth is not an option.

This earth and the current heaven will pass away to make room for the new heaven and earth (Revelation 21:1). Do not be deceived, examine yourself and consider if you will be a vessel of honor or dishonor. Will you be a bondservant to Christ or a slave to the ecstasy? Will you allow sin to be your king and ruler over your being, or allow Christ to redeem your time and life?

This life is not forever and tomorrow isn't promise. When the Lord calls you near, don't reject Him or deny the sin that is within you. Confess your sins to YHWH because He already knows. When we acknowledge our sins before Yah we see how filthy we are and how much we need a savior to save us from ourselves. When we recognize the despicable persons we are, have become—can become, we are like Paul and the Lady caught in the act of adultery.

We see and understand we have been forgiven much so we purpose in our hearts to give our all to Christ. We choose to be a bondservant of Christ willingly laying down our life. We are not a slave according to man's system but joint heirs to the promise to live eternally with Christ our Lord.

Escape the lie that the ecstasy is the pill you want to take to ease your fears, problems, and help you forget your sins. Trust that the Lord is able to pick you up from where you are and set you where He wants you no matter what man thinks! A stripper can be redeemed, a drug dealer, a thief, a murder, pastor, adulterer, liar, gluttons, and the more! His grace, precious blood is sufficient to cover and wash away all sin!

"Deny the Ecstasy and Chase your Destiny!"

ABOUT THE AUTHOR

Growing up Dr. Krystal Lee, known as Author K. Lee has always been adventurous in writing, production, business and being a die-hard entrepreneur. She puts her heart into every project and operates in excellence because that is the standard. She completes every project as if unto Yeshua (aka Jesus) and so she regrets nothing.

K. Lee is a strong believer in prayer and believes the Truth sets anyone free. She is grateful that the Almighty has come into her life. He has removed her from a path of self-destruction then set her on a path to keep her heart, mind, and desire set on helping others. As a kid she wanted to be caviler, not wear her heart on her sleeves, and not cry when she saw others cry. This, however, was not the way the Lord made her.

The Lord called her to have a heart that cares for others. Sympathizes with the afflicted, seeks justice, and helps the needy. K. Lee is passionate about projects that build up people, removes oppression, pain, and delivers hope. Her ambitions as a child was to express her thoughts and those of the silent in music, dance, theater, but especially in writing.

Dr. Krystal Lee has written several books both fiction and non-fiction that she desires to publish during her lifetime. In addition to writing books, K. Lee is passionate about video and media production. She started writing music, then transition to screenplays and theater. K. Lee is a talented singer, actress that prefers to be behind the scenes; she loves to tell a good story.

In addition to her creative talents, she is an entrepreneur owning several businesses. She has established Krystal Lee Enterprises and developing many more. She is also partnered with TUG Outreach, a non-profit organization that helps youth and adults by creating programs and offering services to help the masses.

Dr. Krystal Lee is equally passionate about ministry as she is with commerce, entertainment, and writing. She enjoys teaching and speaking on subjects relative to her life experience and anointed ability. She is a ordained Chaplain with International accreditation and she is in training to walk in her calling of being an Apostle. She believes Adonia (The Lord) has a calling on her life to be a mouthpiece for the Lord to those she is sent; she is prepared to follow His voice and travel to where He sends her without the slightest hesitation. Most of her ministry is online and published on Instagram, Facebook, and KLEProductions.com

K. Lee hates religion, spreading faith through fear, and believes in the value of men no matter their current condition. No one is beyond the healing hand of YHWH if they want the help. Help can be offered but must always be accepted, which requires choice.

Yeshua (aka Jesus) is her Lord and savior and she looks forward to His coming. The days we live in reminds her, the second coming is growing near. She believes and is passionate about helping all that have an ear to hear, hear the Good News.

Connect with K. Lee:

AuthorKLee.com
Facebook.com/KLeeCoach
Instagram & Twitter: KLeeCoach
Facebook.com/KLEPub
The Lesson Program & Materials: KLETL.com

To purchase books and to learn more about KLE's Publishing division, please visit www.klepub.com

To learn more about Krystal Lee Enterprises' projects, programs, events, and media please visit KrystalLeeEnterprises.com

To reserve K. Lee to speak
Call 770-240-0089 Ext 4
Email: KrystalLeeEnterprises@Gmail.com
AuthorKLee@Gmail.com

Mail Request:
Attn: Krystal Lee P.O Box 1635 Conyers GA 30012

Order Books by K. Lee & Other Authors at KLEPub.com for special pricing. Need help with your Book, Script, or Play? We Publish, Ghostwrite, and Edit. Call 770-240-0089 Ext 1 to Learn More!

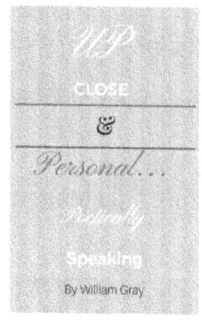

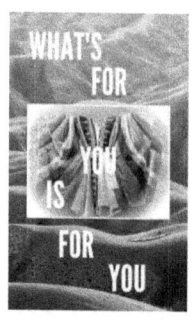

Order Books by K. Lee & Other Authors at KLEPub.com for special pricing. Need help with your Book, Script, or Play? We Publish, Ghostwrite, and Edit. Call 770-240-0089 Ext 1 to Learn More!

www.ingramcontent.com/pod-product-compliance
Lightning Source LLC
Chambersburg PA
CBHW070545300426
44113CB00011B/1794